W9-AJT-088

J
529
A1    Allington, Richard L
       Beginning to learn about time.

**DATE DUE**

| | | |
|---|---|---|
| SE 20 '85 | AG 07 '85 | |
| NO 23 '85 | SE 25 '85 | |
| JA 29 '86 | | |
| MR 13 '86 | | |
| JY 28 '86 | | |
| APR 23 '86 | | |
| MAY 23 '86 | | |
| DEC 18 '86 | | |
| FE 21 '02 | | |
| JE 28 '02 | | |
| AG 08 '02 | | |
| AG 21 '02 | | |

EAU CLAIRE DISTRICT LIBRARY

DEMCO

# Time

**Library of Congress Cataloging in Publication Data**

Allington, Richard L.
    Time.

    (Beginning to learn about)
    Summary: Introduces basic principles of telling time
and such related concepts as today/tomorrow/yesterday,
past/future, and late/early.
    1. Time—Juvenile literature. [1. Time]  I. Krull,
Kathleen. II. Miyake, Yoshi, ill.  III. Title.
IV. Series.
QB209.5.A44  1982      529      82-10170
ISBN 0-8172-1388-0

Copyright © 1983, Raintree Publishers Inc.

All rights reserved. No part of this book may
be reproduced or utilized in any form or by
any means, electronic or mechanical, including
photocopying, recording, or by any information
storage and retrieval system, without permission
in writing from the Publisher. Inquiries should
be addressed to Raintree Childrens Books,
205 W. Highland Avenue, Milwaukee, Wisconsin 53203.

Library of Congress Number: 82-10170

1 2 3 4 5 6 7 8 9 0 86 85 84

Printed in the United States of America.

Richard L. Allington is Associate Professor, Department of Reading,
State University of New York at Albany.
Kathleen Krull is the author of twenty-nine books for children.

# BEGINNING TO LEARN ABOUT

# TIME

BY RICHARD L. ALLINGTON, PH.D., • AND KATHLEEN KRULL

**ILLUSTRATED BY YOSHI MIYAKE**

Raintree Childrens Books • Milwaukee • Toronto • Mexico City • London

90061

EAU CLAIRE DISTRICT LIBRARY

There are many ways to measure time.
A clock measures time.

The short hand
tells the hour.

The long hand
tells the minute.

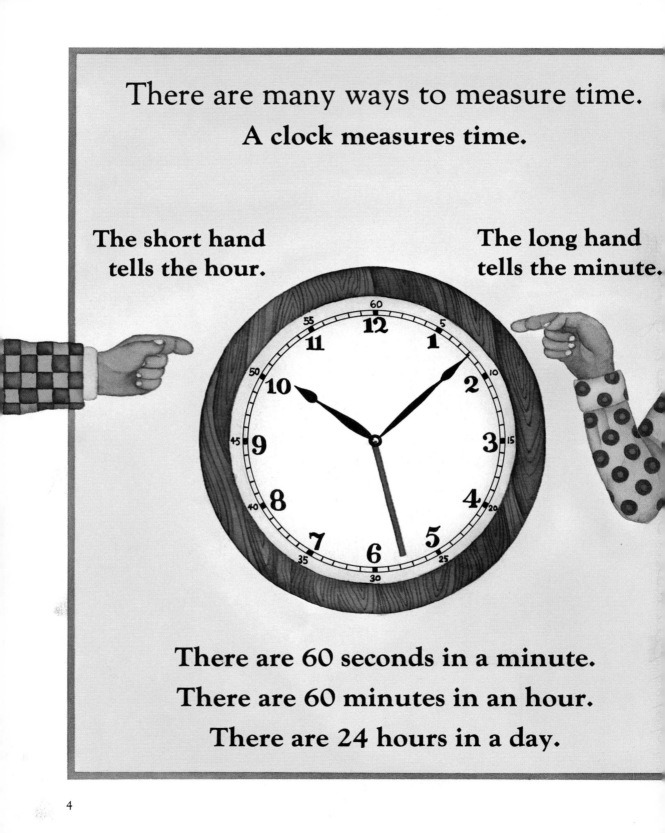

There are 60 seconds in a minute.
There are 60 minutes in an hour.
There are 24 hours in a day.

With your finger, draw a line
between the clocks that match.

Look at these clocks.
What time does each one show?

As you read the rest of this book,
look for these clocks. Say what
time it is on each page.

Yesterday was Sunday.
Today is Monday.
Tomorrow will be Tuesday.

There are seven days in a week.
Can you name them?

It's the first day of spring!

There are four seasons in a year.
Can you name them?

We draw pictures about March in art class.

There are twelve months in a year.
Can you name them?

MARCH

| S | M | T | W | T | F | S |
|---|---|---|---|---|---|---|
|   |   | 1 | 2 | 3 | 4 | 5 |
| 6 | 7 | 8 | 9 | 10 | 11 | 12 |
| 13 | 14 | 15 | 16 | 17 | 18 | 19 |
| 20 | 21 | 22 | 23 | 24 | 25 | 26 |
| 27 | 28 | 29 | 30 | 31 |   |   |

13

EAU CLAIRE DISTRICT LIBRARY

Time goes so slowly when
I'm waiting for lunch.

When does time seem to go slowly for you?

Recess goes by much too quickly.

When does time seem to go too fast
for you?

Sometimes I don't even notice
time passing.

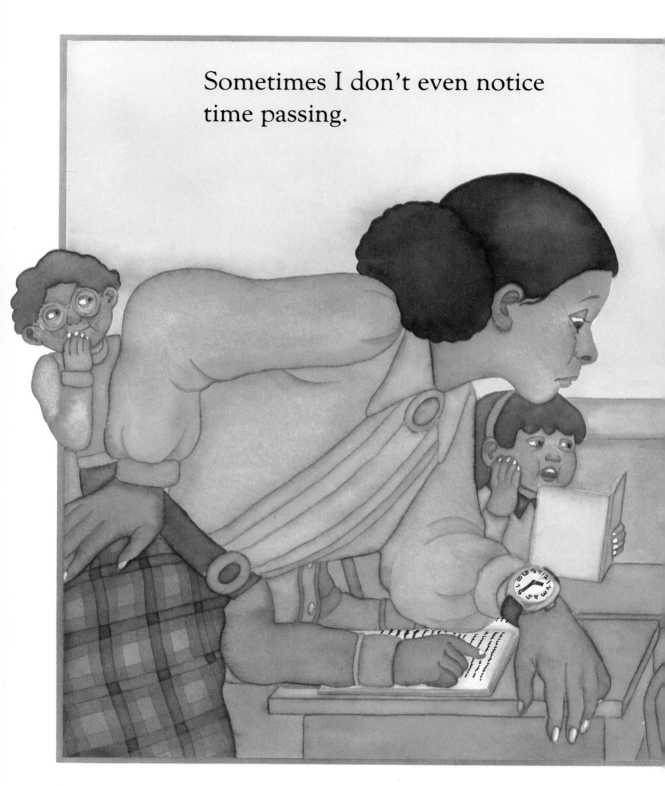

Are there moments when you don't notice time passing?

In science class we learn about things
that happened long, long ago.

What does "long, long ago" mean to you?
Make up a story about something that
happened then.

For homework, we have to read a story about the future.

Make up a story about something
that you would like to do in the future.

"There's no time like the present,"
Dad says. "Never put off till tomorrow
what you can do today," Mom says.

What old sayings about time can you think of?

It takes me so long to clean my room
that I'm late for my favorite TV show.

*What things do you hate to be late for?*

Every night I write in my diary.
I put down what has happened
during the day.

March 21,   Monday
Dear Diary,
Today was the first day o
spring.   I fell asleep in
schoo      sh I coul
have       all d
Afte       no
rea
a

Tell someone about what you did today.
How many things can you think of?

I had to clean up my room
and it took me so long
that I almost missed my
rite TV show.
hardly

SODA

I like to read for an hour before I go to sleep. Sometimes I can finish a whole book.

How much time do you spend
reading each day? How long did it
take you to finish this book?

Make your own book about time.
Look at a newspaper or magazine.
Find as many pictures of clocks
as you can.
Cut them out, and tape or paste them
onto pieces of paper.
Fasten the papers together.
Tell someone a story about what you do
at the different times your book shows.
You may ask an adult to help you.

Think of something you can do in

**one second**

**one minute**

**half an hour**

**one hour**

**one day**

EAU CLAIRE DISTRICT LIBRARY